THE FALL INTO SIN

Genesis 2–3 for children
Written by Nancy I. Sanders
Illustrated by Joe Van Severen

Arch® Books
Copyright © 1996, 2004 Concordia Publishing House
3558 S. Jefferson Avenue, St. Louis, MO 63118-3968
All rights reserved. No part of this publication may be reproduced, stored in a retrieval system,
or transmitted, in any form or by any means, electronic, mechanical, photocopying, recording,
or otherwise, without the prior written permission of Concordia Publishing House.
Manufactured in Colombia

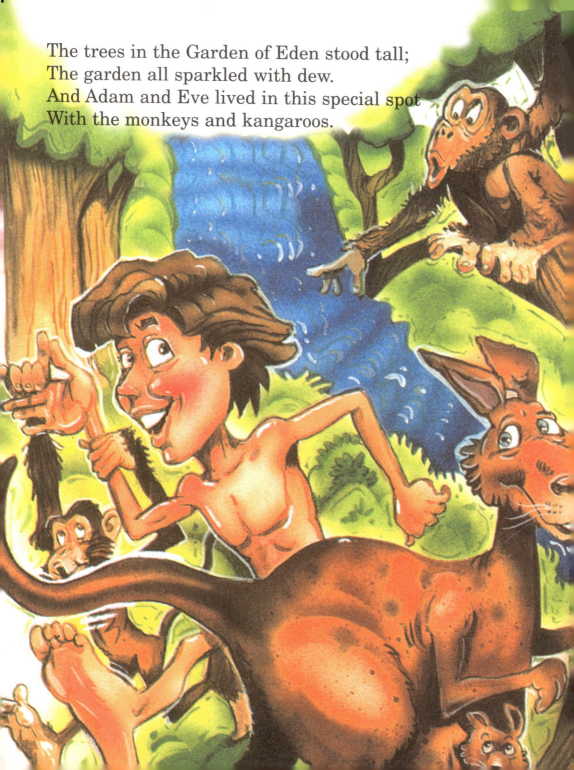

The trees in the Garden of Eden stood tall;
The garden all sparkled with dew.
And Adam and Eve lived in this special spot
With the monkeys and kangaroos.

The Lord came to Adam and Eve one day,
He said, "Since creation is done,
You're free to eat fruit from the trees that you choose."
God pointed, "Except from this one."

And Adam and Eve saw the one special tree
Of knowledge of evil and good.
And God said, "If anyone eats of its fruit,
He'll die. It is not meant for food."

Now life in the Garden of Eden was fun!
The lion cubs played with the lambs.
But wait! Look! A sly, sneaky snake
Came hissing along through the sand.

The snake hissed and whispered to Eve in her ear.
He asked her, "Did God set the rules?
Did God really say that you can't eat the fruit
From this tree? Oh, don't be such fools!"

Then Eve answered back to that devilish snake
(Who really was Satan disguised),
"Why, yes! God told Adam and me not to eat
The fruit of one tree or we'll die."

"Ha, ha!" laughed the wicked old snake. "That's a lie!
I know what will happen to you.
You'll see whether something is evil or good
When you eat a piece of that fruit."

"Delicious!" Eve said. "This fruit's really good!
And look, I did NOT die right now!"
She shared bites with Adam and started to ask,
"I wonder why it's not allowed?"

Then Adam yelled, "Yikes! You're naked! Me too!"
For suddenly they'd become wise.
"Oh, no!" Eve cried, "I hear God walking near!
Quick! Hurry! Oh, where can we hide?"

"Where are you, My children?" God called as He walked.
And Adam cried, "We're hiding here.
We heard You and hid because we felt ashamed.
Our nakedness caused us great fear."

So God said, "Who told you that you wore no clothes?
Did you eat the fruit of the tree?"
Adam said, "Eve said I'd like how it tastes."
And Eve said, "The snake deceived me!"

Then God took the evil that Satan had planned
And changed it (as only God could).
He said, "For this sin, you'll eventually die,
But wait! Here's a promise for good.

So God showed a new home to Adam and Eve
Away from this life-giving tree,
And angels with flaming swords stood guard
From people who might try to eat.

So Adam and Eve and their sons—and *their* sons—
Each struggled with hard jobs to do.
And people worked on as they waited for God
To make His great promise come true.

Then one starry night, a sweet baby was born,
Christ Jesus, God's own promised Son.
Through Him God forgives us and makes us His own,
And gives us the life Jesus won.

Dear Parents:

After hearing this story, it is natural for children to want to blame Adam and Eve (and Satan!) for all their troubles. They may self-righteously claim, "If I had been there, I wouldn't have eaten that fruit!"

Explain that Adam and Eve, as the first people God created, are something like our first mother and father. Point out how easily we give in to temptation and sin every day. If we had stood in the garden, we would have done exactly the same thing. But stress the fact that God does not punish us for our sin. On that day long ago when sin entered the world, God promised to give us the gift of a Savior—His Son— to suffer the punishment for our sins.

When the time was right, God sent Jesus to live, die, and rise again to win for us life with Him, now and forever. Take time to pray with your child, confess your sins, and thank God for His forgiveness. As God covered Adam and Eve's embarrassment and shame with clothing made from animal skins, and He covers us with the love and righteousness of His Son.

The Editor